Paths of the Soul
Alpha

Abridged edition.

PATHS OF THE SOUL
Alpha

Edgar Boone

Soul International Media, LLC
2014

Copyright © 2014 by Soul International Media, LLC

All rights reserved. This book or any portion thereof may not be reproduced or used in any manner whatsoever without the express written permission of the publisher except for the use of brief quotations in a book review or scholarly journal.

First Printing: October 2014

ISBN 978-1-942386-00-1

Soul International Media
5 Southside Drive, Suite 335
Clifton Park, NY 12065
www.pathsofthesoul.com

To Keith Raniere.

"I am of the opinion that my life belongs to the whole community and as long as I live, it is my privilege to do for it whatever I can. I want to be thoroughly used up when I die, for the harder I work the more I live."

– George Bernard Shaw

PREFACE

6 August 2014, 10:05 AM

The material I'm publishing in this book is, of everything I have written, the closest to my heart and the most meaningful. It is because it represents a very important transformative stage in my life (2004-2009).

During this period, I spent a lot of time studying, thinking, introspecting and exploring the inner realms of my mind. There were days in which I would spend twenty hours a day studying reality - from the foundational concepts of time and space, to the general laws of physics.

I also studied systems in biology, computers and businesses. I studied other human activities like war and organizational strategies. I learned about mental illnesses, sociopaths, how our body dies and near death experiences.

I learned about different eastern spiritual paths and western psychological explanations to our human struggles. I explored the nature of our three dimensional world and the possible existence of a fourth dimension and beyond.

But more than anything, I intensely looked into the nature of thoughts, and the space within which they exist.

Without knowing I was developing a great capacity for concentration that led me to be able to control my mind, to keep it still. Through this process I seem to have discovered the realms in which thoughts exist, where energies move, where our spirit resides.

In time I also learned to manipulate my mind's space. I learned to move it, shape it and guide it. I discovered that this space was actually a living thing! A living energy!

This living energy expanded gradually through my physical body, my mind, and beyond. It expanded through what some eastern philosophies call chakras or energy centers.

When this energy flowed to the first chakra, I felt a type of explosion that created with it a unique experience of life. It was like putting glasses on from which I could perceive reality.

I also felt as if I was being hooked to a strong, raw, electrical current. It was very painful, but I learned that if I stabilized the energy, the pain would diminish. I also learned to amplify or decrease its intensity.

As soon as I stabilized the first chakra, I experienced an explosion in the second one, and then the third, and on and on. With each, a new perspective and experience would come; with each, I went through the struggle to learn to control it. With each, I saw the world with new eyes.

As the energy flowed and increased, my mind's space expanded to cover not only my whole body, but all of reality. The line between the inner and outer world disappeared, becoming one living intelligence, of which I was part, but also "It."

Many of the realizations I was having were related to the nature of the universe, what we are, and how we work. At the time, I was not that interested in money, relationships or things. I just wanted to discover the source of creation.

And this journey led me to find it, to find what seems to me is the source of it all. In my writings, I call this "All," "The Beginning And The End," or the "Alpha And The Omega."

It was then, one summer while I was sitting exploring this inner space that I felt a rhythmic type of heartbeat that didn't seem to come from my physical body. I connected with it and realized, it was a higher aspect of me or what I would call my soul. My poetry in this book series is very much a dialogue between "me" and It.

In the beginning as you will read, it was not an easy relationship. It wasn't because the "me" of that time felt threatened by the presence of something or someone else within. But the more we got to know each other, our relationship grew into a friendship, and then into something like a lover's union.

During these years I used to play volleyball on a consistent basis. I used the sport as a training vehicle to strengthen my body, my emotions and my mind's capacity to concentrate. I also used it to practice increasing and stabilizing as much energy as I could hold.

One night as I was practicing stabilizing the chakra on top of my head while playing a game, I experienced myself stepping out of my physical body. I got out and went up, up through a hole that led me to another world. It was beautiful! It was sublime!

This moment was the culmination of years of inner work, years of practicing mastering the energies of every center. It was a triumph and a huge step for my journey back "home."

Through this process I became more and more private. I learned quickly to not share what I was going through, because when I did, some people would often react with fear or denial.

I contemplated for years wether to publish this book. I knew that it would be controversial, specially with those attached to a traditional view of reality. At the end, I decided to take this book public because I believe it can serve as tool to those on the path of Self realization.

I hope this book can also serve as a reminder that we are so much more than what we think we are and that we are part of something far vaster and deeper than what we are aware of.

I also believe it would be good for all to know that, in order to discover and build the light in us, we need to go through the fire of facing our darkest aspects.

This book describes part of what this fire has been for me. It does so in poetic form, describing, metaphorically and literally, the paths I have traveled.

Keep in mind as you read that I didn't write these poems with the intent to publish them. I wrote them as an expression of my most personal and vulnerable moments; I wrote them to help my rationa mind discover aspects of myself that it wasn't aware of. I wrote to document my process.

Everything I have shared here represents my own personal views, and not those of any person or group with which I may have been, or am, associated.

Before you start I also would like to share with you that I don't consider myself a poet, or writer, per se. I see myself more as someone who feels deeply and who has been tempered by this fire.

This is the first book of several others that I will publish in the future, where I describe my stages following 2009.

With love,

Edgar Boone

Thanks

I am very grateful to my mentor and dearest of friends, Keith Raniere. He has been by far the most influential person in my life, especially on my journey of Self-realization and growth. His example has been an ongoing source of inspiration, his training a vehicle for self mastery, and his guidance a compass through the darkness. Without him, I would not be the person that I am today.

I'd also like to thank my parents, for when I was a child they inspired me to search within and without. They opened my mind to the existence of much richness beyond a conventional life.

I also would like to thank Mariana Musi for her enthusiasm and work in the publishing of this book. She took the material I had hand written, from 2004 to 2009, and studied and organized it in such a way that we were able to discover its different lines of thought or themes. This book is a compilation of one of these themes.

Lastly, I thank Dan Bratman and Sean Craney for their editing work, as well as Ken Kozak for the art, layout, and design of the book, and Megan Mumford for the book's cover.

– Edgar Boone

How to read this book

I'd recommend that when you read this book for the first time that you read it in order. The reason for this is that the collection of poems is really one poem, one process that you discover as you go.

I'd also suggest that in the beginning you simply experience the book, rather than trying to understand it. Then reading any poem individually may deepen your experience and understanding.

Note from the Author

In this book I refer often to the divine. Sometimes I use words like God, Lord "The Source," or "All" to describe it. I also use other terms like "Presence" and "Intelligence." I write referring to names of people or "Gods" from different cultures. The words I use are not meant to profess a specific religious belief, but to express, to the best of my ability, my experiences.

Throughout the book there is a back and forth dialogue between different "aspects of the Self" or viewpoints. They oscillate between an "I" or "Me," a "higher Self" and "God." This book is a dialogue between them, as they go through a process of transformation and union to become One.

Some people may see this path as spiritual and others as a psychological relationship between the conscious and the unconscious in all of us. No matter what point of view you may choose, this book can be read as a process of union and love.

Introduction

For thousands of years we as a race have been questioning and exploring what and who we are, how we shall live, as well as our existence. These explorations, for many, become journeys traveled on the way to the realization of Self. The book that you are about to read is the story of one of these journeys, one that is still in progress.

– Edgar Boone

Edgar Boone

May 20th, 2004

What's the matter?
Why are you upset?
Why do you question yourself so much?
Why are you waiting? What are you waiting for?

If there was no death, what would you do?
Are you waiting to die, so that you could live?
So you are destined, so you have chosen!
Do you forget dear one?

From the realms of the unknown
The shapes of the known come about
To land in your mind and into the world

But I feel tired, weak, ashamed
Angry and depressed
No longer wishing anything
I feel short lived
I am still doing the same things I used to do
Isolated from friends, people, myself and the world

Dear one, confused you are
but honest you have been
In the transition you can and may remember
The beauty of the universe, of you, of others

Letting yourself down may not serve you best
You continue to choose things that are not good for you
Are you seeking answers here? Writing, reading? In your mind?
Where is your heart? Where is your laughter?

—m—

May 20th, 2004

There is no time in what you are
There is you and who you think you are
In the mist of the fog
Sometimes you forget

—⁂—

July 10th, 2004

Would you say hello to me if I call your name?
Would you care to come and be born?
Would you care to join me in this fabulous adventure called life?

Would you care to say
OHM

Would you care to call my name?
Isha

In ecstasy I dwell and swim
Oh Lord

Would I lose consciousness of you if I sleep?

—⁂—

August 28th, 2006

Oh my Beloved
In my heart you live
Outside, I thought you were
Until I saw

In me you were
Oh my Beloved
I've been chasing a shadow
Oh my Beloved
Oh Beloved
Beloved
Beloved I am
I am

—⁂—

August 29th, 2006

Knock, knock
Who's there?
Don't know

Knock, knock
Who's there?
Didn't I tell you? Don't know

Knock, knock
Who's there?
Is there a something knocking?
Oh! Knocking something is!
What is that?
Oh! Related to me?
What is me?
Me is who I am?
And I, is what?
Don't know

Knock, knock
Who's there?
It's me, the "I"
Whatever that is

Knock, knock
Who's there?
It's me, your beloved friend
Your new discovery
Your new friend
Your you
Your I

Knock, knock
Who's there?
It's me
"Me" welcome you are
Thank you for coming

—m—

September 16th, 2006

I feel the burning of love
I feel the sensuality of living
I feel the joy of perceiving
I feel curiosity for our universe
I feel wonder for my existence
I feel

—m—

Edgar Boone

December 7th, 2006 – 2:34 a.m.

In my deepest being I feel you
Beloved creator
As a thick space
You fill me
You surround me
Exploding in joy and happiness
I am in your eternal presence

—⁂—

December 14th, 2006

Essence that permeates all
Because it is all
Thick substance in movement
Containing love
Giving compassion
Penetrating each molecule of my being

In you
I am wrapped and I dissolve
In you
I discover and recognize my Self
You are all and nothing
Silent intelligence
Total witness
Experience of the eternal process
Always becoming
Something unpredictable
And conceivable
Oh, sweet magnificence
Base of my soul
My heart rests in you

Tired of the duality fight

Opening my eyes to love
Nurtured I am
And strong as a lion I guide your children
Raising the curtain of their ending illusion
Placing them in your arms
For their transformation
Thank you for our existence
Creator

—⚍—

December 16th, 2006 – 2:40 a.m.

Oh beloved one
Beauty emanates from your eyes
Windows to your nurturing soul
From which rays of love
Illuminate our hearts
Wisdom to our minds

Oh beloved one
Grateful we are
Of you coming alive
Songs and laughter
You brought to our lives

Oh beloved one
You touch me softly
Like a rose caressing my heart

—⚍—

Edgar Boone

December 20th, 2006 – 1:19 a.m.

Oh beautiful child
Loved you are
With all my heart

You inspire in me
The deepest sense of beauty and love
You are a carrier of light for my eyes

Through clarity
You shine the path
Of those who will come and be nurtured
By the food of your heart

Oh beautiful child
Loved you are
By those around you
Those you have touched

With the softness of your hand
You birth beauty in everyone
Bringing them close to you

Oh Beautiful child
Loved you are
By every angel in heaven and earth
That rejoice in your smile

—m—

January 4th, 2007 – 3:27 p.m.

In All and in Nothing
You are
How can I say that something could not be
If you and I are
How can there not be if all is
Oh dear
I only desire to deepen in you
To know you
To be amazed by you
And love you
Unknown known
Eternal presence

January 4th, 2007

I only want to increase my capacity to know you
To admire you and desire you
To live in you and with you
And never rest of wanting to see you and hold you
To be in you and with you
This is what I recognize
Nothing and no one
Not even death or ignorance
Could ever keep us apart
Illusory solitude
Never existed
It was just me
Who couldn't see you
And recognize you
Oh my beloved

You are All
I know no more
I enjoy my existence
As I am the eyes of your presence
My senses belong to you
As a window to our world
Created by you
And only in you
Nothing more than you
Death is only
Of my ignorance

January 4th, 2007

Come to me my beloved
Rest in my arms
Repose in my heart
I've waited eons for you
Now you are back to me
With a humble heart
Here I receive you
To never leave you
As what has been earned
Can never be lost
All your descendants
Will enjoy of your essence
And benefited they'll be
Of your existence
Forgive me for having left you
Reunited we are
Here and now
In the eternal moment

January 4th, 2007

Give me the key that opens your heart
That I really want to see it and be naked in it
Eternal tenderness
I bathe in you
I bathe in the universe
To come out rested
And beloved forever

―⚋―

January 4th, 2007

Will you be there when I wake up
from this long dream?
Oh my beloved
Will you be there when I come back
From the long road of ignorance?
Will you be there when I look for you?
Will you be there when I arrive?

But I have never left
And you have never departed
In my presence
You've always been
Only in your dream you had left

―⚋―

January 4th, 2007

On my road
I've been discovering
Sparkles of your existence
Through my questioning and observation
I have found you
And I can't but admire you
The unknown/known
Eternal presence

—⚡—

January 13th, 2007

Oh Humanity
I hear you cry
I hear your prayers
Asking for help
Asking for solutions
To the problems
Of your own creation

Illusionary happiness
Unreal creations
Prisons of ignorance
Heavy and guilty

Joy in this life
It's possible
Here I am

—⚡—

January 16th, 2007 – 3:30 p.m.

Eternal existence
Eternal presence
That covers it All
That is All
Without understanding I perceive
And in my perception I delight
Of your sensual movement
Oh what pleasure to be alive

—⁂—

January 19th, 2007

I feel sadness
I mourn my own death
The death of an illusion
The illusion of death itself
For what is death but a birth?

Will I miss my old self?
No
I am grateful
For the sacred space inside of me
Grateful for the blessing I've received

I cry as a statement
Of who I am
And who I thought I was

—⁂—

Edgar Boone

January 19th, 2007

I am dying
I am dying slowly
I can feel it
But not understand it
I am dying
I am dying slowly

We could say it is our fate
With every step I move closer to death
More peaceful I've become
It is worth it

January 19th, 2007

I am in the void
I am inside the bubble of emptiness
I am floating in the universe
I am nurtured by it all

January 28th, 2007

Who?

Eternal witness
Always present

In peace
In joy

You exist

The will
Born from you

The mind
Your direction

The body
Your instrument

We are alive

—⚭—

January 28th, 2007

In my veins
Your substance runs
Giving life to my soul

If I would see you again
And find my self in your presence
I would melt by the intensity of your sight
That goes through my matter
Revealing to you
Every secret of my existence

Oh my Beloved
Destroy my pride
That limits my experience of your presence
Alive essence of existence itself

Let me die in you, in your arms
Take me to the other world
That only you could show me
Oh beautiful one
My beloved
Benevolent and real
Beautiful and intense
Let me die
To be reborn in the world
That only you know

Direct my path
And transform my fear into perfume
To guide those in the path

Oh Beautiful one
Please let me die
To be reborn in your arms
With total trust in the eternal life

Oh my Beloved
Existent in an unreachable future
I have dreamed and adored
An illusion's image
Obsessed in finding you
You
Who wouldn't allow
To be revealed

If we could merge our hearts
I would dissolve into you
Creator
Revealed in every particle
Revealed in consciousness itself

January 28th, 2007

Observer and observed
You've shown me that by observing I've been created
And
I've died by observing what had been observed
Who I was no longer exists
And who I am
Is a question

—⚍—

January 28th, 2007

Observer, is that what I am?
Is it you I've been looking for?
Is it you I've longed for?

Is your love the one I've dreamed of?
Are you my beloved, the one I have missed?

You have always been there
Covered by a delicate veil
That didn't let me see you
See your essence

Affectionate and alive
Playful and defenseless
Proud and powerful

Enjoying existence

—⚍—

February 6th, 2007 – 9:52am

From the eternal presence
Colors are born
From the eternal presence
Sound is born
From the eternal presence
All has come
And here I am
Having the experience
Of the never born

February 6th, 2007 – 2:10 p.m.

I hear angels singing
I hear angel's music
My heart opens in joy
The beauty transfigures my mind

The pure and loving beings
Bring light into my life
Dear friends
Welcome to my home
I am humbled by your greatness
And honored by your presence
Welcome to my home

February 10th, 2007 – 4:23 p.m.

Voices, I hear voices
Subtle voices in my head
Sweet voices that speak to my heart
Voices of courage
Voices that sing
Voices that talk to me like a friend
I have a lot of friends

—⚬—

February 10th, 2007

I hear voices
Voices of sorrow
The cry of humanity

I hear voices
I hear your cry for help

Oh, humanity
I hear your screams
I hear your loud voice
Asking for help

Oh humanity
I hear you
I hear your voice of anger

I hear your voice
A single voice
Of all humanity

I hear you, loved ones
I hear you

Come to my arms and rest in peace
Feel the comfort of my presence
And recognize that it was all a dream
Just a dream

—⁂—

February 14th, 2007 – 1:15 a.m.

Silence, oh silence
Enchanted I am in your sound
Constant vibration

—⁂—

February 14th, 2007 – 11:00 p.m.

I feel you through my body
And I hear your voice
A silent voice of wisdom
That has no words
Says nothing
But says all

Intelligence in movement
I can only sense you
But not understand you
I feel peace when I connect with you
I float over you
You carry me through life

—⁂—

February 19th, 2007 – 10:42 a.m.

Rest in my arms and feel my peace
From the never created
All creation comes

Our minds and hearts become one
Lose yourself in me, to become who you are
In the trust of the Self, you will die
Only to be reborn into my eyes

—⚏—

February 19th, 2007

Would you come to me to say hi?
Oh loved one! Of feminine one!
Would you come to caress my heart?
Would you come and melt my mind?

Please take me with you
To never come back
To this place of roughness and separation
Please open my eyes

—⚏—

February 19th, 2007

I am tired
But it's not physical
I seek rest
But not for the flesh

—⚏—

February 19th, 2007

I am the source of all wisdom
I am wisdom
I am All
And All is I
The source and the created
The father and the son
Nature and the sun
I am the Source

―⁂―

February 19th, 2007 – 5:00 p.m.

I feel my arms being born
I feel my heart being created
I feel the metamorphosis of becoming

―⁂―

February 23rd, 2007 – 5:09 p.m.

I see
I know
I breathe
I breathe fresh light
I know I am

―⁂―

I seek
No thing
I give
By existing
I am

―⚬―

May 2nd, 2007 – 1:35 a.m.

I wonder when I talk
Who's talking?

When I touch
Who's touching?

When I hear
Who's hearing?

When I see
Who's seeing?

When I taste
Who's tasting?

When I smell
Who's smelling?

I wonder

―⚬―

May 20th, 2007 – 10:40 p.m.

Sweet essence
Fills my heart
My empty void

It opens my eyes
To see the beauty of it all

I feel compassion
Compassion for my fellow men

I want to be of service
I want to be a channel

For eternal evolution

—⚜—

May 26th, 2007 – 10:14 a.m.

Come to life and let's be friends
We are brothers on the path

Come to me, my child
That you have to live
Resting upon you
The lives of others are

Be wild, be crazy, be you
Take in your nourishment
Of prana and light

—⚜—

June 1st, 2007 – 11:03 a.m.

Strip away my body
And let the soul be born
Out of thunder
Out of effort

Let there be light
Let there be joy
Here I am
As a proclamation of my existence

—◊—

June 2nd, 2007 – 11:03 a.m.

Shiva
My lover

You melted my heart
You melted my mind

Here with open arms
I'm fusing with you

Destroying my old self
I am coming about

Grateful I am
For being alive

—◊—

June 2nd, 2007

I am alive
I am afraid
I am in this animal
But I am more than it
I am

―※―

June 11th, 2007 – 9:03 a.m.

In love and in war
With a human struggle, I strive to survive

In sorrow and in joy
My human soul sought to be whole

But one day
At the coming of the dawn
A realization came about
Completion has always existed
Confusions were a memory veil

Here, the ultimate joy
The ultimate realization was achieved
My soul is free

A new path has begun
A path of expression and creation
A path of enjoyment and depth-ness
An experience of being All

―※―

June 14th, 2007 – 12:33 a.m.

My desire to save the world is gone
My desire to help people is gone
My desire to please is gone
My desire to be liked is gone
Some fear is still present
What's next?

―⁂―

June 19th, 2007 – 12:30 a.m.

Comprehending to be
An awareness in consciousness
The Self is realized in the heart of God
The deep sea of consciousness
The place of it All

In that moment
All is revealed
Well, almost all
But it really doesn't matter
All desire is gone

―⁂―

June 19th, 2007

The universe is at your service
Because you are the universe

So wonderful boy
Wonderful man
Come alive

Spread your wings
Fly to the sky
And let the sun melt your heart
That its rain
Will bring us to life

—⁂—

June 19th, 2007

Hear my voice
Feel the vibration
Feel the Universe
Feel alive

—⁂—

July 20th, 2007 – 2:24 a.m.

Oh Silence!
Through you I perceive
The mysteries of existence
Through you I feel
The grace of being alive

—⁂—

July 20th, 2007

Where was I
But lost in a sea
Of random thoughts

Running from the ghosts of my mind
Illusions
Monsters of the body
But where was I?
Isolated from it all
Starving in front of a feast of love

July 20th, 2007

Your light
Shines through darkness
Transforming
Hopelessness into inspiration
Suffering into joy
Ignorance into wisdom
Isolation into humanity
But most of all
Apathy into caring
Grateful we are of your existence

July 22nd, 2007 – 12:13 a.m.

I have arrived to a place I did not expect
A place I never dreamed of
Because what I've dreamed was an illusion

I have arrived to an unknown place
Full of peace and presence
It feels so familiar and so unknown
I know everything but I know nothing

Edgar Boone

I feel the essence of existence
The purest love, I feel scared
It's different, it's new

I have arrived
Where have I been?
I have the strong impulse to destroy it

I have arrived!
But where?
But to a stepping stone
On the way to so much more

―⚊―

July 22ⁿᵈ, 2007

Welcome
You are home, she says
Welcome back

―⚊―

July 22ⁿᵈ, 2007

I arrived
As usual
It is not what I imagined
I see in front of me a path
A path of compassion
A path of love
Love for mankind
The melting of myself into God

―⚊―

August 1st, 2007 – 3:02 p.m.

I am grounded in it All
Here,
All is
Here,
There is no movement
Here
I am that I am
And from that mystery
"I am"
Is expressed

August 22nd, 2007 – 1:55 a.m.

I do not seek power and I do not seek fame
I do not desire and I do not despise
I do not seek and I do not give up
I do not control and I am active
I do not lust and I am passionate
I am not happy and I do not suffer
I do not think and I am alive
I smile and my heart is at peace
I struggle, yet my mind is still
In fire I live
In water I rest

August 22nd, 2007

Rest in the palm of my heart
Listen to the sound of silence
This sound of love, the sound of all

Edgar Boone

The silence screams in my head
This silence and this peace
Are more intense than anything I have ever felt

The intensity of it all
Expressed in this beautiful silence
The ever-eternal silence

—⚋—

August 22nd, 2007

This Silence
Louder than any sound
Is gentle and powerful
It touches me
I can see it
It is me
It is all

—⚋—

August 22nd, 2007

In other realms I am
In other times I am
In other spaces I am
In here I am
And there I am
In you I am
And I am in you

—⚋—

August 22nd, 2007

Language
Product of the mind
Bridge to the eternal

Fire to the bridge
I dissolve in the All

―᳁―

August 22nd, 2007

You are being seen
You are being thought
How could you be alone
With the company of your own presence
The loving and all eternal

―᳁―

August 29th, 2007 – 3:32 a.m.

I have died, I am empty
When I was not there
"I" was transformed
Peace arrived
Then "I" came in
A new me
A universe in itself
A wonder to be discovered
Clay to be molded

―᳁―

Edgar Boone

August 29th, 2007

No where to go
Nothing to do
I exist
And that is all

Awareness in stillness
Consciousness in motion

I am here
In this place
Where peace is striking

August 29th, 2007

Come as you are
Gentle heart
Come as you are

August 29th, 2007 – 10:42 p.m.

I am the flesh
But I am not it
I am my mind
But I am not it
I am you
But I am not
I am I
But what is that?

When I stop the question
I is only I

—⁂—

August 29th, 2007

Am I an abstraction?
Or am I real?

When I think of me
I have an idea of me

When I experience
Someone is there

When logic dies
Only "I" is there

—⁂—

August 30th, 2007

In the practical I live
In the subtle I exist

—⁂—

August 31st, 2007 – 10:14 a.m.

Yes, you are in love
How could you not?
But to love existence

Edgar Boone

With a body full of fire
Desiring it all
Merging with All
Shaping it All

—⚏—

September 1st, 2007 – 3:30 p.m.

Heavy flesh
Light spirit
Struggle in place

—⚏—

September 1st, 2007

I wake up
I am aware
I am in struggle

I am in this body
I am the driver
This heavy car
In motion it likes to be
And in rest it wants to stay

My companion, my friend
We have our ups and downs
We are lovers
We are friends

—⚏—

September 1st, 2007 – 4:56 p.m.

You open your eyes
I say to you
Thank you for coming

Thank you for inviting me
I like being here
Here with you

Thank you for your invitation
The invitation to your home
It's warm and it's cozy

Now your heart is my mind
And my mind is your soul

Grateful I am for our marriage
Together we'll always be
Till we merge into the All

—⁂—

September 1st, 2007

Do you want to come?
Do you want to join?
Do you want to descend into existence?

I'd like you to come!
I have missed you for so long
I had forgotten your existence
Drowning in my longing of you
Beloved one

Edgar Boone

I had lost
What I didn't know I had
I have remembered
I want you back
You are welcomed in my home
My heart awaits you
My mind is empty

Come as you please
And let yourself be
To express and enjoy
The creation of your being

I'll join you in your place
As I have missed you too
In your travels I have been
But distracted were you

I have arrived
I am home
Yes
I accept our marriage

Let's make love
Let us merge
Apart we will never be
The longing is over
This struggle has ended
We are stronger now
Now I am in love

I am here, I am here
A being to humanity
A brother to my race

A fellow traveler
A friend to you all
I am here
To destroy and to build
To transform and to shape
To mold and to play

—⁂—

September 2nd, 2007 – 2:02 p.m.

I see
I see fullness
I see life
I see

I feel power
I feel love
I feel

I hear the sound of silence
I hear one voice
The voice of humanity
I hear

I taste
I taste the flesh of life
I taste

I smell
I smell the essence of it all
I am alive

—⁂—

September 12th, 2007 – 12:30 a.m.

    The will of the Father
    Accepted by the Son

September 12th, 2007

    Let the world tremble
    Let the world shake
    Let the world hear
    Let the world be humbled
    By the one voice
    The sound of change
    The sound of power
    The song of humanity
    Om

September 12th, 2007

    Let there be joy
    That I am here
    Let's celebrate life
    As how could we not
    But rejoice in living
    As we do in dying
    All is the same

September 12th, 2007

Angels sing
My heart melts
Drums are heard
My body shakes

I exist in wonder
I exist in solitude
I exist
How could I not be?
If I am and I am aware

I am alive
I want to live
Because I've been asleep
I don't want to go back

—⚋—

September 13th, 2007 – 8:10 a.m.

I and only I is
Because what is
Is all there is
And I am That

That which is true
That which is love
That which transcends
That which does not
As all distinctions
Are of the mind

—⚋—

Edgar Boone

September 13th, 2007

Silence
Oh sweet silence
Where no fire and no shape exist
Only consciousness
My heart rejoices
My body fears
Together we live
A human life

—⚟—

September 13th, 2007

Let there be light
I said
And my eyes opened

Let there be sound
I said
And my ears opened

Do I create?
Or do I perceive?

—⚟—

September 20th, 2007 – 5:41 p.m.

In this presence
The silence is loud
Time slows down
I no longer exist

All is All
Effortless
Flowing like a river
Existence is

—∞—

September 20th, 2007

Let's merge
But haven't we already?

Where have I been
But sleeping while you came

Now we are One
And I wonder what That is

—∞—

September 30th, 2007 2:57 a.m.

I am in struggle
I feel fear
I am angry
I seek a refuge
Please save me!
I don't want to die!

But how could you die
If in my arms you are
Asleep you have been
As I have carried you
All this time

Edgar Boone

But I don't trust you
Who are you?
I don't know you

Yes you do, deep inside
You know me

Drink from my lips
Feel my peace
You are home
You do not need to worry
As bliss is your shelter

But so much beauty
Is strange to me
Is it that you want to destroy me?

No
I embrace you
Come along
Merge in my heart
Let your mind be empty
And in love we will always be

I am home

Yes, you are

Thank you

Thank you

Paths of the Soul

September 30th, 2007

Would you receive me
In your heart
After so much arrogance
After so much hate
After so much anger against you
I am ashamed
I don't want to show my face
I don't want you to see me

Oh my dear
So foolish you are
In the eyes of the mother
Only love exists
In the eyes of the father
Only possibilities are

You are welcomed
As you have never left
Only in your dreams
You have been

Carried by my light through the darkness
Alone you were not
In my arms
Embraced you were

Come to me, but don't move
Relax into me
As I am you

Oh, let your Self be
Don't you see?
You have been blind

Edgar Boone

You have not seen love
You have always been surrounded by it
I have always been
I have never not

Now that we are here
Why don't we become one?
You can always leave
As welcome you'll always be

I run from you
But I want you
I fear you
And I love you

It's ok. It's ok.
Whatever you choose
At the end
You will come back to me

Oh, so much love
Reveals my hate
So much compassion
Reflects the stupidity of my thoughts

—⚞—

October 8th, 2007 – 2:03 p.m.

No where to go
Nothing to do
Waiting for the fruit to ripen
In silence
And in noise

In peace
And despair
I want to scream
Shout to the wind
Take me out of this prison
Of my own ignorance

And even in this
"I am" in peace
Yes I am in peace
Experiencing it all
Like a guardian lover
Protecting his offspring
I wait until the time is right
Then thunder will strike
Laughter will be
And power will be

—⚬—

October 9th, 2007 – 11:52 p.m.

I love, I feel
Therefore I exist

I am here and there
I am everywhere

I am the cause and the effect
All the same

Therefore
I am

—⚬—

October 10th, 2007 – 10:32 a.m.

I am that I am
I am and I will always be
In every moment

I am that I am
Because I am

Yes I am
In the dearest of terms
I can say I am

I exist
I have always existed
Because "I" is
And "is" is "I"
So "I"
Is all there is

—⁂—

October 10th, 2007

No here, no there
Only I
No back, no forth
Only I
No yesterday, no tomorrow
Only I

The eternal presence
The OMNI "I"

—⁂—

Paths of the Soul

October 11th, 2007 – 11:26 p.m.

I want to quit
I want to give up
I crawl into my skin
To never come out

Afraid of the world
Afraid of nothing

To realize that nothing
Has been the object
Of my defense

Oh my dear
Come to my arms
Rest in peace
And be strong again

Go back into the world
Back into striving
That my breath sustains you
With life and love

―⁕―

October 15th, 2007 – 3:37 p.m.

I can touch
But not with my physical hands

I can hear your angelic voice
But not with my physical ears

I can see your beauty
But not with my physical eyes

I can smell your essence
But not with my nose

I can taste you
But not with my tongue

You permeate every inch of my being
But I can't relate to you through my physical body
Therefore I am more than my physical body

You witness every action of my being
You are ever present
Ever loving
Ever compassionate
And all knowing

October 18th, 2007 – 1:54 a.m.

I want to fly
I want to be free
I want to break through

October 18th, 2007

I hear the music of the Gods
I see the colors of the angels
I smell roses
I taste the spices of God
I am alive
I live

October 18th, 2007 – 9:00 p.m.

Let the drums play
The rhythm of my heart
That I'm going to war
As I am a warrior
Destroyer of illusion
Bringer of light

Let us hear the flutes
That my heart rejoices
Let the trumpets play
That life as it is
Has melted my being

I have become aware
Lets celebrate
The arrival of the Son

―⚬―

October 19th, 2007 – 8:10 a.m.

The love of effort
Has taken me to the highest delights

The desire for comfort
Into hell

The passion for striving
Has taken me to the beauty of the Self

And the desire of the flesh
Into prison

Edgar Boone

I am aware, I see beauty
I am conscious of my existence
I am in love with the world

—☆—

October 21st, 2007 – 5:02 p.m.

In stillness,
I know all
In stillness,
I experience true love
In stillness,
only awareness moves
In stillness,
my power exists
In stillness,
I exist
As I am still
In all points in time

In stillness,
I can perceive beauty
In stillness,
I am compassionate
In stillness,
I die
In stillness,
I am reborn
In stillness,
I fully express

Oh stillness
I am in you

—☆—

October 26th, 2007 – 3:07 a.m.

I am the observer
I am the witness
I am the presence
I am All
I am That

—◊—

November 2nd, 2007 – 2:39 p.m.

I am no longer what I was
I am in love
I am love
I am
I

—◊—

November 5th, 2007 – 9:41 p.m.

Like a forest burnt by fire
Only ashes remain of my old self

Through these ashes
I can remember
Patterns of the past imprinted

Now I am here
Stepping into my memory

I see a self that no longer lives in me
Though is so much a part of me

I am
But do I really?

I am
But who?

I am

Yes

I am

I am I

I am the cause
I am the effect

Here I am
Over there I am

I am
I have always been

—⁂—

November 9th, 2007 – 1:30 a.m.

In me
You have become
You have let go

In my memory you will always be
Sleep forever
In the eternal now

—⁂—

November 12th, 2007 – 5:19 p.m.

Rest in peace
Receive what you have earned

The heart is open
The mind is quiet

The world is love
Magnificence all around

I am nowhere
I am no one

―⚬―

November 13th, 2007 – 8:14 p.m.

You see through me
You speak through me
I am an instrument
An instrument of the soul
A beautiful angel
Full of compassion

―⚬―

November 15th, 2007 – 10:47 p.m.

I love my body
I desire through it
I love with it
I wonder through it

I love my body
I make love with it
I sleep in it
I move with it

I love my body
Wonderful tool
Tool of expression

Through it
I let others know my thoughts
But mostly
I know myself through it

I love my body

Yes

I love my body

—⚊—

November 16th, 2007 – 9:59 p.m.

I feel the thunder of your voice
Sound of the Gods
Vibrations of love
Swirl through my spine
Culminating in the most exquisite orgasm
The opening of the Eye
The all seer
The all knowing
The giver of peace

In which I am reborn
To become a bringer of peace
A bringer of Joy

―⚋―

November 17th, 2007 – 11:37 p.m.

I feel the pain of your sadness
I can feel the suffering of your longing
I can feel the pressure of your burden

I'd like to set you free
Welcoming you
Into the warmth of my arms
Where you can rest
Where you can cry
Where you can let go
In liberty then you'll go
And I'll watch you fly
Flying back to the depth-ness of your soul
To come back reborn
Bringing words of wisdom
And peace for us all

―⚋―

November 19th, 2007 – 3:18 p.m.

I feel pressure
I feel pain
The pain of being alive
It hurts but it's good

―⚋―

November 19th, 2007

I speak through this body
I see through these eyes
I am alive

—⚜—

November 19th, 2007

Why do I exist?

Who am I?

Where do I come from?

—⚜—

November 22nd, 2007 – 12:28 p.m.

To push
To strive
To move forward

To rest
To be
To do it again

—⚜—

November 22nd, 2007

The angels sing
They rejoice
In the wonderful marriage of the soul

Now all together, like a chorus
They sing your song
The song of God

The waves travel
Creating all things
All circumstances
I only need to hear
To focus on you
Then I remember

Oh yes
So good, I remember
Who I am
And where I come from

I'm being transformed
Into an angel
Beauty and goodness
Of a gentle spirit
With a heart that brings together
All human souls

—⚎—

November 25th, 2007 – 11:25 p.m.

I want out!
I want to be free!
From the burden of my own sins
My pride
Big as the moon

—⚎—

Edgar Boone

November 28th, 2007 – 12:42 p.m.

I fight, but I can't win
I surrender, but I can't give up

I continue on a path
That leads nowhere

If I don't move
I won't go anywhere

The purpose, none
The reason, why not?

Anything else?
Well, I am here

—⁂—

November 30th, 2007 – 10:28 p.m.

I yelled to God
My voice came out like thunder
Screaming, saying,
I have the right to be!
To exist! To express!

I yell to you
I am angry
I'm not angry at you
I am angry at my own lies
I have been lying to myself
I've lied that I have not lied

Oh! I hear the truth now
I rest in it
I am in peace
Now, here
I feel the intensity of your love
Power that destroys the veils of separation

Oh! My lover
I never thought I'd get home fighting
Through it, I learned to love
Now I flow like a river
And I roar like a lion
I am soft as a baby
And sharp as a warrior
Thank you my God

—⁓—

December 7th, 2007 – 9:46 p.m.

I am dead
All that I know is gone

Who I am?
Don't know

Where is "I" going?
Don't know

Where am "I"?
Everywhere

My intuition
Covers all known and unknown

Edgar Boone

I have let go of the fight
I have surrendered

I am merged in love
We have become One

—∞—

December 7th, 2007

Consciousness
Like a stream
Continues to flow

The thoughts are settling
I perceive in slow motion

Space
Became a swimming pool
A pool in which I move

The water is a deep silence
A very loud silence

I feel the density of my muscles
I sense the structure of my bones
I see all light crisp and intense
My senses are sharp

There is only the now
With a few jumping thoughts

Like two lovers
The two worlds are merging

Like a flirting couple
There's a push and a pull
A coming and going
In the deepest passion of existence

—⚜—

December 9th, 2007 – 7:43 a.m.

I am in the flesh
I am an animal
I want to mate

I want to eat until my hunger is satisfied
I lick my fingers

It is good to be here
What else can I do
With this beautiful instrument?
With this mammal animal?

—⚜—

December 9th, 2007

I'd like to jump
I'd like to dance
I'd like to make love
And sing
I want to play
I want to fall
I want to experience pain
And the softness of a lover's skin

I am alive

—⚜—

Edgar Boone

December 16th, 2007 – 1:40 a.m.

Take me to the point of no return
The place where only silence exists
Where time slows down
There, my heart opens
There, my heart sings
There, my heart rejoices
There I am free

No more strings
That bring me back to delusion
To fear
To ignorance

I want to lie there
Where I will be reborn again
Where I and only I will exist
Where there is no room for doubt or fear

There is only me and you
Only we
The ever-existing

OMNI ALL

―⚞―

December 23rd, 2007 – 5:54 p.m.

Sing my brother, sing
Open our ears to hear
The sound of truth

Speak my brother speak
Words of wisdom

Let our minds gently receive
The food to grow our soul

—m—

December 28th, 2007 – 8:27 p.m.

Cry, cry my child
Your tears of impotence
Your tears of anger
Your tears of sacrifice
That, that life is over

A new age has begun, an age of joy
A time of harmony and expression
It's time to come back home
We have been waiting
Your education is just starting

I am to be in the world
Let humanity merge in my heart
Let them rest in peace
That my struggle hasn't been in vain

Freedom to all, is
The door is wide and open
The vision is narrow
Let those who can see, walk in
And let the blind wait for their time

Time is changing
Movement is accelerating
Change is inevitable
Suffering could be minimized

Edgar Boone

Let the door of our homes be open
For those in need
For those who seek
And to the ignorant ones

That one spark of light
Could open their eyes

Then
The blind will see
The mute will speak
The crippled will run

—⁂—

December 28th, 2007

We are here
In freedom and suppression
Contraction and expansion

Two forces against each other
Merging into a wider struggle
Merging into the galaxy

The in-breaths and out-breaths of God

Until one day
Only stillness will be
But not eternally
Only for a time

Then
The world will be born again
We will all come back

—⁂—

I am that I am
Because I am

—⚬—

December 31st, 2007 – 2:15 a.m.

The thunderbolt of my anger
Travels through my veins
It burns my flesh
It leads a yell
Words of a fighter
Words of sadness
Words of a tired one
From all the wars fought in vain
The voice says
I won't take it anymore
The bullshit of the world
The common lies
And subtle suppression
That gently kills
The innocent ones
I won't take it anymore

—⚬—

January 2nd, 2008 – 11:08 p.m.

I long for a loved one
I long for a long warm hug
I long for a warm caring body next to me
I long for your sweet lips to bring me peace and calm
I long for your smile to tame my tiger

Edgar Boone

I want to open my heart
Don't you see?
My body is burning
It is on fire
It is at war
It is going to war
I fear for the destruction that will come
But it needs to come
Yes, as gentle as possible
But it will come

The walls will crumble
The truth will come out
It will cut sharply those who deny it
And it will be a sweet elixir
For those who desire it

Don't you see?
That's why I am here
To transform and to build
To break and reunite
A stronger force
A purer humanity

—⚏—

January 7th, 2008

Oh sweet elixir of peace
Where have you been all of this time?
I have longed for you
I have been in hell
I have been lost

The pain
Has been there all the time
The vibration
Too intense for me to handle

Oh, then I discovered
I could take the energy out of the wall
The wall that separates heaven and hell
Sweet and bitter
Once it went through the hole
I was able to rest
You see, my longing for a beloved
Was a longing to be at peace, to rest

My body has been burned
My mind dismantled
My consciousness rising
But still not fully in place
I have been lost, confused
Nervous, angry and in fear
Now, I want to rest
I feel like crying
This struggle is over

—⚡—

January 7th, 2008

I am whole
But lonely
I am one with all
But lonely

Edgar Boone

I can feel humanity's struggle
But I am lonely
I see what they can't see
More lonely

I can feel what they are not even aware of
And I am lonely

I feel connected to all
I am all and I am no one
I feel lonely

I have had little joy in my path
It makes me wonder the futility of life

January 8th, 2008

Your tender lips touched my heart
The beloved and the lover
Have become ONE

Now the beloved
Are all human beings

January 8th, 2008

My heart is at peace
My mind is calm
My eyes see beauty
I perceive possibilities

The universe is deep and full
I swim in it
I have become
I have remembered

What sweet experience
That of truth, that of stillness
From which
I experience the source

God, the body, the full body
What is beyond you?
Who knows? But for now
I am complete

—⚞—

January 11th, 2008 – 1:06 a.m.

God

You think me
I am part of your body
I move
Towards you

Towards integration

All is understood
All is known
We are One

—⚞—

January 11th, 2008 – 1:06 a.m.

I feel pain
I am exhausted from fighting
From striving
I don't want to come out of your being
I want to be there all the time

—※—

January 13th, 2008 – 4:14 p.m.

I am here
In presence and in flesh
In consciousness and in mind
In emotions and in action
I exist

—※—

January 13th, 2008

I was
But I never knew what that was

I sought
I longed for something
I guess to be reunited

In my seeking
I found

What I thought "I" was
Started to die
To fade away

Then she arrived and took her place
As she grew, then he came
With her compassion and love
With his power and directness
I was born

I am the son

—⁂—

January 14th, 2008 – 7:15 p.m.

I feel tension in my body
Like a bridge about to be broken in two

The energy flows through me
Like a million volts through a cable

I want to jump out of this flesh
I want peace, I want to release
I would fight with anybody near

—⁂—

January 18th, 2008 – 2:24 a.m.

I can see, I can hear
But I am blind and I am deaf
I hear silence, I see Darkness
I feel water but I live in "solid"

—⁂—

Edgar Boone

January 19th, 2008 – 2:26 a.m.

I have died
But I came back
I do in fury
Fighting for my right
Until she comes
And melts my heart
I can not but surrender
To become One

—⚏—

January 20th, 2008 – 12:37 p.m.

The presence merges into the flesh
Obscurity and light come together
Giving birth to a wonderful being
This star, this Godlike figure
This, all seen, all loving
This, I am, as I am THAT

—⚏—

January 20th, 2008

Surrender and go on
Fight but don't destroy
Build as you go

—⚏—

February 8th, 2008 – 12:30 a.m.

I am
Because I am
And will be
In presence
And in soul
I am
The source
And the effect
I am

―⁓―

February 12th, 2008

I crawl into my skin
I want to die
I scream
I want out
Out of my own prison

―⁓―

February 13th, 2008

With you my heart opens
And rejoices
Singing in harmony
Becoming one with the angels

―⁓―

February 16th, 2008 7:04 a.m.

Oh Lord, Oh Lord!
Thank you for the gift of life
Thank you for this opportunity to experience

Thank you for my journey
I transform
I grow deeper
Closer in you

February 21st, 2008 – 12:14 a.m.

I am the love of the world
The light of knowledge and wisdom
I am

March 13th, 2008 – 7:30 p.m.

Open your mind to your heart
Open your heart to your mind
In this wonderful marriage
The angels rejoice

March 13th, 2008

Oh Lord, Oh Lord
That which created me
I feel your power in my veins
I feel your compassion in my heart
And your laughter in my mind

You will, I act
I will, you act
Partners in the tango of life

March 13th, 2008

Distracted I have been
Lost in the flesh
Fearful of truth
And eager to the pleasures

Oh
I'm here now
Oh yes
I am here now

—⚬—

March 25th, 2008 – 4:35 p.m.

You come, you go
Lost in poverty, lost in wealth

Inner knowledge
Ready to be discovered

Oh brother, I hear you cry
I hear your prayers for a different world

You wonder
Is the purpose of existence to suffer
To experience pain, to lack

Oh dear
Lost in perception
Lost in the senses

It's only a game
A puzzle to be solved

Edgar Boone

One to enjoy
One to figure out

―∞―

March 29th, 2008 – 9:09 p.m.

I have no words to explain
The unspoken wisdom
The source of it all

How can I put into words
The experience of the presence
The experience of my soul

How can I put into words
The freedom experienced
The un-worded wisdom

How can I paint the pictures?
Of the inner stars of my being
Of their constant motion
Of their magnetism
How can I?

I live in several worlds
One of silence
One of darkness
Where I hear the source of sound
Where I see the beginning of light

But could I express
The music of the angels
The winds of the Self
Can I?

Oh you!
Oh me!
Oh we!
There's no one and one

Oh
My heart melts in love
My mind is stupid in the things of the world
I live in ecstasies and I live in fear
I live in joy and in worry

I live in two worlds

—⚜—

April 7th, 2008

Oh my dear
You cry
You suffer
You want peace
Your longing won't be long
Please let me merge into you
To become one
The struggle of merging will be over
You will rest in eternity
Experiencing the joy and beauty of the Gods

—⚜—

April 9th, 2008 – 10:50 p.m.

My mind wanders
Sometimes it drives me into hell

Edgar Boone

My heart aches
Sometimes it is lonely and in sorrow

My body pains, it seeks peace
Is it worth to struggle through life?

To push?
To experience more tension?
To be alone in a crowd?

Is it better to be stupid?
Is it better to be mediocre?

Sometimes
I'd prefer to go back
Pretend I don't know

Push, push, push
Drive your mind towards the dream
That when you get there
You will be disappointed

Don't push
In there you will find death in laziness
Is there another way?

Yes

Don't fight
Don't run away

Strive!

April 13th, 2008 – 5:45 p.m.

I am full
I am in love
As is my nature
I feel I
I live in I
I move through and in I
I see only I
Hear only I
I am
I

―∞―

April 13th, 2008

I see so much
But I am blind
I hear so much
But I hear mostly silence
I feel so much
But I'm not there
I am there
And everywhere

The world dances
I am still
The world changed
I do not
The world is still
But it's only I who changes
We dance together

―∞―

Edgar Boone

April 23rd, 2008 – 1:34 a.m.

The solid still presence of my love
Explodes from my heart into you,
Merging into One
Dying into nothing
Reborn I have been
Into the unknown of my being

—⚏—

April 27th, 2008 – 5:00 a.m.

Come kiss my face
Take me home
That I'm tired of living!

—⚏—

May 25th, 2008 – 5:48 p.m.

In the struggle
I have been burnt
I feel hurt
Hurt of what?
What has been hurt?

Oh this delusion!
Oh this dream!
Sometimes so real
Sometimes so distant

I only long to go back to the source
Oh delusion, oh dreams!
So real, so intangible

—⚏—

May 25th, 2008

Let there be death
So that I can be re-born
In the nature of truth
In the nature of love
The nature of all
The One

May 25th, 2008

If you cry in your longing
If you suffer in fear
And you feel separate and alone

Remember that you are not
Deep inside of you
Your truest and deepest friend is talking
Just step in and listen

Sweet words of love and truth
Let them take you back to your Beloved
Let your self die
Merge into me

May 26th, 2008 – 1:20 p.m.

Thunder struck
He fell
He's burning

The flames are reaching high
As high as the moon

As deep as the universal heart
His longing has been heard by the angels
Peace is available
For the broken one
If we could only open him a little
Only a little

For him to see the light
To hear the music of his soul
To experience the tears of joy of his friends
And hear the laughter of his Self
The surrender of his pride

The time is here
It is now
For the soul to reign upon the human castle
The temple of God

—⚯—

June 8th, 2008 – 5:42 p.m.

My body is in pain
It burns
It shakes
It trembles

The world is falling under my feet
There is nowhere to run
Nothing to grab
Just nothingness

In the midst of everything
I am alone
But I am not
The vibration travels
Through every cell of my being

I am dying
I am dead
The fear
Goes away

Only peace and pain remain
The intensity of the feeling pushes my skin
It stretches all boundaries of my being

No understanding
No
Nowhere to go for answers
Just me and this experience of…
Who knows?

Is this what life is about?
Pain, struggle
Is it that we are here to experience?
Loneliness, Fear, Suffering?

Is this the meaning of life?
Some say no!
Some say human beings are beautiful creatures
That we are loved beyond measure

But where is that?
I do not experience it!

I do not feel it!
In me, there is agony

I scream to the universe
"What is this all about?"
Is this a joke?

The answer came:
You may say what you want
But the nature of the universe
The nature of what and who you are
Does not change

The beauty of being
Is only perceived by a still mind
The struggle of living
Is only endured through love

Yes
Love and faith

The trust
That we are One

There is confusion
In loneliness and fear

You see you are and you will always be
A part of me

My beloved son

Fear not
Cry not
You are in my heart

You just don't see it

June 17th, 2008 – 2:45 p.m.

Oh humans!
So hurt and so lost
In the drama of creation

Oh loved ones!
In the process of your birth
I have been with you
In every step
In every moment
In every thought

I am in you
As you are in me

You see
I am you as you are me
I open my arms to you
Come to me, blend into me

My brothers, my sons
Dissolve your delusions in me
So that you be born again
Born into me

―⚋―

July 24th, 2008 – 2:00 a.m.

In pain I live
Through this body
I express

Through it
I enjoy the struggle of living

In it I have died
In it I've been reborn in spirit

I am a sparkle of God's creation
A pattern formation of God's will

I am nothing but That
Though in essence
I am He and He is me
I am in this temple of God

—⚬—

July 27th, 2008 – 2:50 p.m.

Love
Burns like fire in my heart
Propulsion towards creation

Love
Bliss that gives me peace
And raises my struggle of living

Oh Body, Oh soul
Together towards union with God
Death in the nothingness
The ego has died
Has it?

Will I be able to hold
Against pressure
Against pain
Against pride

Take me where I'll die
To be raised high
Towards the angels
Singing praise to it All

—∞—

August 2nd, 2008 – 12:19 a.m.

If you cry
I listen
If you are in despair
You are in my arms
If you are lost
It's only in your mind
As in my kingdom
All is in ME

—∞—

August 3rd, 2008 – 10:00 p.m.

Open your eyes
See what's there
See your Self
See the truth

Let my beauty
Melt your heart
That its truth
Will make you a man

—∞—

Edgar Boone

August 4th, 2008 – 9:55 p.m.

I love dearly and deeply
I am in love with creation
How could I not?
With so much beauty

I experience compassion
As how could I not?
With such a struggle

I experience anger
How could I not?
Having this body
Failing to move so many times

I experience fear
As so much is unknown

I experience excitement
As there is so much to grow
To ponder upon

—⚡—

August 10th, 2008 – 11:58 p.m.

I am
I am here
I exist
I am the I
The All in the I
And I in All

—⚡—

August 13th, 2008 – 3:00 a.m.

One breath
One mind
Living in unity
Flowing as a river flows

―⚬―

August 16th, 2008 – 9:25 p.m.

Love me
Take me to your heart
Where I melt and become ONE
You see, I've missed you too
Now I am home, yes I am home

―⚬―

August 19th, 2008 – 10:55 p.m.

This flesh,
Yes this flesh
Such a vessel in this world
With this flesh
I come and I go
With this flesh
I feel and I talk
Yes, through this flesh
But is it really flesh
Or is it just an idea?

―⚬―

Edgar Boone

August 26th, 2008 – 1:55 a.m.

I see only shadows
These are days of darkness
In which even the sight of light is painful

These are days of anger
Of fear, of confusion

These days, yes, these days

Will they ever be over?
Will they ever end?

—⚜—

August 27th, 2008 – 2:13 p.m.

I see the dance of the world
Coming and going
Laughing and crying
Birth and death
Success and failure
All in the mind

Now a new vision arises
The union of all
Humanity as a being

—⚜—

August 27th, 2008 – 2:13 p.m.

Senses
Windows to my soul

Oh what presence I experience
When I go beyond
When I let go

When "I" die
Self is born

—⁂—

August 29th, 2008 – 3:16 p.m.

The essence of love
Brings joy to my heart
The doors of heaven
Open up
I go through
The air is crisp, electric
The smell is sweet like a rose
I float around and open my eyes
Such beauty in every atom
Such dance of all beings
It's nice to come back home
And realize the forever truth
Of what I have always been
And what I am
The Ever-Present

—⁂—

August 29th, 2008

Rise
Yes rise to sky
Go to heaven
Reach the stars
Mingle with angels
Sing along
The praise of it all
Then come down, come to us
Bring yourself down
To a place where we can talk
Stay with us, until we can hear you
Until we can see you
Then bring us together
Holding hands
Merging into one

August 29th, 2008

I am a song
A song in motion
A symphony of God
Growing towards perfection
In the process of becoming
ONE

August 29th, 2008

I am here
I hear sounds
Does that mean I exist?

If I can see the beauty of the world
Does that mean I exist?

I feel
I feel pleasure and pain
Does that mean I exist?

Is it me the one that is talking?
Or is that just my mind?
Is the ever present blissful Consciousness "I"?
The All of it All?

Oh! I drop this wonderful mind
Now is the only time
Here is the only place
Existence is all there is
And I am all
As all is I

—⁂—

August 29th, 2008

The silence is here
It's the background of all sounds

The feeling of my body
Takes me into a sensual realm
The realm of the senses

I feel present
I feel alive
I rise

I see the blissful union
Of the ugly and beautiful
Of the grotesque and sublime
Creating this consciousness of being

The One and only One
Dancing, vibrating, breathing, transforming
Moving without moving
Changing in no time
Pulsating, giving birth to all, to us
To all sentient beings

August 29th, 2008

Oh
Oh yes!
Yes, I am conscious
I am the Father
I am the Son

August 29th, 2008

You come, you sit, you ask
Looking for answers
Longing to be back home
To the place of warmth, of safety

You don't want to leave
You want to stay forever
But you can't, you need to go

—⚏—

August 29th, 2008

I feel pain in my body
I'm angry
When is this going to stop?
This burden of being alive
Pain and more pain in every movement
Why is this so?

—⚏—

August 29th, 2008

Die in peace my friend
Your job has been done
Rest with the angels
I'll take it from here

—⚏—

August 29th, 2008

I feel shallow
I feel my body satiated, tired
Wanting to drop dead
But no
I'll stay, I'll strive
I'll move forward

—⚏—

August 29th, 2008

You tell me you love me
But I can't feel that
You tell me let's be joyful
But I don't know what that means
You tell me let's dance
But I can't move
You ask me what's wrong with you?
And I say I don't know

I don't know where I am or who I am
But I see you and hear you
But I don't know who you are
Turmoil sets, in my body
My eternal companion

Now I open my eyes and I look
I see beyond my eyes
And see only rainbows of light
I can hear the loud noise of silence
All others seem distant away

I can feel nothing
But I can feel beyond feeling
My inner being lights up
It shines, it moves forward
It is being born
It is coming alive!
It wants to dance!
It wants to break through!
Speak up and scream!

I AM ALIVE
I EXIST
ONLY BECAUSE I SAY SO
I AM AWARE

NOW
YOU DO EXIST FOR ME
AS I CAN FEEL YOUR VOICE AS MINE
I CAN FEEL YOUR PAIN AS MINE

I hear your prayers asking for help
I have no more to give you
But my own body
My own heart
Rest in it, die
Now together we rise
To the highest delights of being
THE EVER PRESENT
OM
THE EVER PRESENT
"I"

—⚜—

October 22nd, 2008 – 1:28 a.m.

Time stopped
My heart beats
My sight focuses on no thing
Only darkness is visible
An infinite world
There's nothing to observe
But the All
I am some thing and All
I am All and some thing

—⚜—

Edgar Boone

April 19th, 2009 – 12:10 a.m.

The waters are calm
The captain is waiting for the right moment to sail
The wind is quiet
I can see the storm, but it is far away
It is approaching, but still not here
The sun shines
The body is recharging
The mind, adjusting
The soul is healing

—⚡—

April 24th, 2009 – 1:28 p.m.

No one can see me
But I can see them
In this inner prison
I have discovered my freedom
Beyond space and time
I travel through the mind of God, my mind
I have just discovered my adolescence
Eager to reconnect with my elders
Ever present but recently discovered

—⚡—

May 1st, 2009

The planet breathes as I breathe
It moves as I do
It cries as I do
It prayed for help, I came

It is struggling, I am
I am the world
I am Humanity

I carry the karma of my brothers on my shoulders

—⚋—

May 18th, 2009

The waters were calm
They moved peacefully
Recharging the all-mighty force

Then the storm arrived without warning
Hell broke loose
Old structures were destroyed
Nothingness came in
With its attached companions
Doubt and Fear
All moved, all was shaken, I couldn't keep centered
I was destroyed, the self-perceptual "I"
What a loss! What a cry!

I found myself homeless, guru-less, friendless and reasonless
Emotions came like upward fire
The anger, the angst, the fear, the hate
They were burned to ashes
Leaving a mark on my face

Then peace arrived in the unknown, the nothing
Nothing left to lose
Not even reason
Not even the ego could win this fight

They gave way
They are sleeping

—⚞—

May 18th, 2009

The Giant awakes
She has seen the light
She has reconnected with her brothers
She is the bridge between realms
She has come, she has arrived
She is here, she came to stay
To embrace

—⚞—

May 18th, 2009

Let there be lust, lust of life!
Let's make love
Let's create a new world, a new life
Let's create a paradise in this world
A pathway to the spirit
Lets become fully conscious
A human/divine

—⚞—

May 20th, 2009

"I" lived
"I" died
In giving up all
I've gained it all

—⚞—

May 25th, 2009

Oh Lord
Oh my lover and beloved!
Oh dearest of my dearest
You are so close to me
That I can not see you

You are the basis of every sound
But I can't hear you
You are beyond touch
But you are everything

In this rapture of ascension to your heart
I died
And I was reborn through your out-breath
So that I may represent you on earth

May 29th, 2009

Now, she is asleep
The beautiful giant
He is asleep as well
The fearless warrior
The newborn cries out
It is alive and kicking
Cognizing a new world

June 7th, 2009 – 1:00 p.m.

Oh Love!
Worship of the Gods
Substance of the Universe!
So much I am you that I don't know you

I have died in you so many times
And I have risen from the dead
Triumphant like a hero
Only to fall to the ground
Like a scared child
Losing faith, trust and all sense of beauty

But you
You are never away
With a subtle blow of your breath
My chest starts pumping again
Bringing me back to life

Yes, I am alive!
I am alive!

June 7th, 2009

You touch my heart
My pride dissolves
I rise like an eagle
I see the whole
I have risen from the dead

June 7th, 2009

My eyes have changed
They have evolved
They see beyond matter
They are merged
The eyes of the human and the soul
Became one

I see light
I see darkness
I see the past
And I see the future

I see people's pain and suffering
I see their essence
Their true nature
Their potential

I can feel their confusion
I can feel their desire

To be God realized

―⁂―

June 12th, 2009 – 9:20 p.m.

My heart aches
It starts pumping when you are near
My legs become weak
I get nervous
The fear of facing reality
The point where the unknown becomes known
That's the birth of my soul

―⁂―

Edgar Boone

June 15th, 2009 – 9:04 a.m.

I look at the light
My body and soul unite through the vibration
We become One
It's so empty but so full
So shallow but so deep
Someone died
But who is to be born?

―ɷ―

June 15th, 2009

The heavens await
The arrival of one
Which brings with him
A great triumph
That of the soul
The transcendence of the animal
The path of the prophets
The path of the seers

―ɷ―

June 19th, 2009 – 5:50 p.m.

Present and aware
I experience longing
A deep desire for love

Love is like water
I am a very thirsty man

―ɷ―

June 19th, 2009

I long
I desire
I am in pain
I wait for that which will never come

My soul, still in prison
Ignorant of the human ways
Together we ride
The journey of man
The way of the thirsty
Towards the source

I Am that I Am
The answer to your longing
My Beloved
Lost you have been

Now
With the feminine spirit
Open your eyes
Don't you see?
You have always been loved?
Use me to open your heart
Your journey has been long
The way has been hard
You have failed
But you have risen
Risen from the dead so many times

Tears come from my spirit
In the presence of a great one
One who doesn't know his own greatness

Let us begin the melting and merging
Of the highest spheres in the galaxy and soul

Yes
The galaxy and soul

Your next step
As an adolescent of the universe
Here we are after the graduation
A path needs to be chosen

To live
To be
To support
To allow
To teach
To learn
To love
And to forgive
Riding together
We will always be!

—∞—

June 21st, 2009 – 9:25 a.m.

With a broken heart
A beaten body and mind
I am crippled
Literally, crippled

With a messy instrument
I cry, I cry
I am broken

But in this act of love
With this broken heart
I have risen as a human
And I am crippled

I have been lost, I'm confused
But slowly becoming a butterfly
My broken heart is healing slowly
Yes, slowly, but healing

Hate, fear, anger, confusion
They have been close companions
As they melt away through an opening
A little opening that lets some light shine on
That's enough for me
As the nectar of love fills my being

I aspire to be a good lover
But I am still crippled
Oh love, the essence of our beings
Come, melt me away in the final rhapsody
The triumph of the love hero
The one who surrendered everything
Who realized that he is love
That he is love
So I die

—⁂—

June 22nd, 2009

No wonder, no mind
No hate, no love
No courage, no sadness

No joy, no depression
The land in between
The hardest of all

―⚊―

June 28th, 2009 – 11:58 a.m.

Oh God!
Your rays of love follow me
They touch my heart
I am yours

Oh Dear, rest in my arms
We have become One
Channel and recipient
Lover and loved

Long the journey has been
We are married now
Together
Relax into the flow
Open your eyes and see
Open your ears and hear
Reality is our playground

―⚊―

June 30th, 2009

The gates of heaven opened
The energy flows through my being
It burns, it is cleansing all the blocks
Where have I been?

I had lost my power, my dignity!
I am back
Ready for a new battle

—⚜—

July 7th, 2009 – 2:41 a.m.

I am an eagle
I fly high in the sky
Proud of my self
Proud of my being
I see wide and deep
Efficient in flying
Effective in my hunting
Bridge between two worlds
Heaven and earth

—⚜—

July 12th, 2009 – 12:45 a.m.

Walking into the forest
The reality I knew became dark
It disappeared
All that seemed familiar melted into infinity

The lower self became fearful, he panicked
He knew he would die
The monsters attacked
It was his last defense

To attack with all might
Until the wise one came
He brought Light

In small steps
The road became more known
But still trials needed to be faced

Walking and walking
Every dragon was met with fear and courage
Every challenge was met with insecurity and decisiveness
Until all monsters were gone

Light shined
Then joy was present
The child became a man
With eyes of wisdom
With scars on his face and body
He knows the hardships of life

Now a wise man himself
Guides the way
For his fellow Brothers

—⚔—

July 13th, 2009 – 12:26 a.m.

Called towards a journey
Called to fulfill my destiny
Afraid I was
Of ghosts, of hidden monsters

My life became unpleasant
Then I chose
To take the bull by its horns
And fight the good fight

I won
But in the end
No fighting was necessary

That was the moment of real triumph
That which goes beyond two opposite forces
That which links to the source
The consistent, the ever-present

In this process
Self awakened
In the ever eternal space
I became aware
Afraid first of this World
Like an alien I felt

With time and effort
I learned a few things
Little to function in this World

―⚡―

July 13th, 2009.

Surrender my brother
Surrender to the highest will
Subtle and peaceful bliss
Let it burn you
Let it continue the cremation of your being
Until only ashes remain of the old
And aliveness of the new

―⚡―

Edgar Boone

July 13th, 2009

I have been defeated
By the ways of the flesh
I have been overtaken
By the tricks of the mind
I, lost and hopeless,
Gave up for a while
With no energy and tired
Of the path traveled
I laid almost dead
In the dark and dry desert
The place in the middle,
The purgatory
Not hell and not heaven
Worse than either of the two

In there
I stayed for a while
With help
And whenever possible
I rested, I regrouped
I became a little stronger
Only to rise again
Full of hate
Troubled I was
By this wicked experience
But helpful it was

In time and stronger
I swallowed the hate to its demise
To let my Light shine again
Risen from the dead
I am back

Stronger and clearer
Tired and troubled
Long way still remains
For my heart to be pure

—⁂—

July 14th, 2009 – 2:23 a.m.

I cry and I cry
Tears fall out of my eyes
Like a waterfall
My chest contracts and expresses
Pouring sounds of deep sorrow
Of sadness, of desperation
I wonder about my sanity
Am I crazy?
Is this all an illusion?

—⁂—

July 14th, 2009

I cry and I cry
It is a deep cry
Expression of my desperation
I scream for my sanity
Am I crazy?

—⁂—

July 14th, 2009

Your lips
Touched the heart of a wounded man
I have come back

—⚍—

July 23rd, 2009 – 1:43 p.m.

The World seems distant
Far, far away
I am present
I hear noise
There are people talking
Sounds of the world
They are not near me
This substance
This presence
This silence
Is so deep

I dwell in the ocean of love
I hear the inner drum
It's synchronizing with the body's heart
Together they pump

I died for a brief moment
For a few seconds
Later I was reborn
With new eyes of light
And a peaceful heart
Taking the body tiger
To the highest delights

—⚍—

July 23rd, 2009

You tell me
Come
Come help your Brothers and Sisters
And I say, why?
When I do
I am met with sword and blame
With lies and deceit
With anger and hate

I ask, is it worth it?
Do they deserve the secrets of the soul?
So I say

Well, it may be that your inner dreams
Projected into the world
Created destruction, turmoil and despair

The reality of the state of the World
Breaks your heart
You know the path
You know what it takes
Connected to the source you are
Why deny your fellow men
The pleasures of a struggled path
Why?

Haven't we guided you
Out of hate, out of fear and despair?
Be slow to judge your brothers
That in ignorance and fear they live
Afraid of you, some are
As they don't know your world

But why would I do it?
What have they given me?
Tell me, so I can judge
Whether the pearls of wisdom should be given

To the thirsty, give water
To the ignorant, give knowledge
To the lonely, companionship
And to the soulless, a connection to the source

You see, that is love
To give and share, even if hated
To extend a hand even if it is cut
To speak truth, even if criticized
To show up, even if killed
Such is the path of compassion
Such is the way of those
Who walk experiencing the eternal, the bliss
With a human painful heart

So we are
Guides on the path
Sources of Light
A way back home

July 23rd, 2009

Rejoice in the choice
As a burden it is not
But a privilege earned
By the traveled path

As you look back
You know the dangers of the road
Many are coming
Looking for signals
They are

Give them clues
That a way could be shown

As you well know

We will
Yes
We will

At one time or another
ALL GO TO THE ONE

And as we dwell
In the Sparks of the All
Still and all moving creator
We will explode again
Into the fun
Of building the universe's canvas
To destroy it and build it again

Such is the
"In-breath"
And the
"Out-breath"
Between them, we rest

To gain strength
To play again
The drama of life

—∞—

July 23rd, 2009

You ask me to go and help you
But when I do, you hate me
Why would I go?
What assurance do you give me of your love?
Why would you cut my hand, when I feed you divine peace?
Why would you ignore divine wisdom?

Oh, lost you are my lover
Lost you are

—∞—

July 23rd, 2009

You ask me to come down to help
To support those who hate me
Those who make fun of me, and criticize me
You ask me to bring down the discoveries of the inner realms
But why my dear, why would I?
I befriend angels and beings
Why come down?

Oh!
My heart is still not pure

—∞—

July 28th, 2009 – 2:41 a.m.

Married we are
Together forever
Two minds
Two bodies
The Buffalo
And the Eagle

August 2nd, 2009 – 5:34 p.m.

The seventh seal was opened
It was of one of the last blows to delusion
The gates of heaven opened wider
I saw the Father with the Guides
I experienced the Holy Spirit
I realized Self
What a moment!
What intensity!
What love!

August 6th, 2009 – 8:14 p.m.

I am the Father
Here is my Son
I will help him grow
Grow and mature

Edgar Boone

August 11th, 2009 – 11:44 p.m.

I am here, I am home
I have settled in this new base
It feels good
From here I will create
I will move the world
I will shake it
It is time

—⁂—

August 11th, 2009

I desired a wife
I no longer do
I desired children
I no longer do
I desired freedom
I no longer do
I desired comfort
I still do
I desired peace
I no longer do
I am at a new place
I'm getting acquainted with it

—⁂—

August 15th, 2009 – 2:12 a.m.

I unplugged
It feels so good
I'm more at peace

Away from the storm of delusion
From the ghosts of the past

I am present
Here and now
I look around
I feel

I am human
I am divine
A hub of realms
An interdimensional man

My time is approaching
As the time has come
To break free
From the chains of time
I am here, I am now
I look around
I am present
I am a hub of time
As time is connected to me
And not me to it

I am alive
The Son
Yes, the Son
I am the Son
As I am the Father
Together we dance
In spirit's water

Edgar Boone

I am here
I am now
I am everywhere
I am at every time
I am consciousness
I am alive
I am eternal
I am ever-present
I am omnipresent
I AM

August 17th, 2009

I saw the light
It was white
It was a bubble
I had fear
I saw
I experienced a presence
It was me
I experienced, experiencing
I am THAT
How do I explain?
I am the Source
Having the experience of being everything else
But I am All
As personal and simple
I AM

August 17th, 2009

The deepest of the experiences experienced
It was so simple
So personal
So profound
So quick
A recognition came suddenly
While listening to music
I became one with it
Fear intensified
I let go of the fear of the fear
Then I experienced
The real I…
Then I turned off the light

August 25th, 2009

In tears I tell you
My beloved
We have arrived
We are home
We have won
We became One
One with All
We are IT

Now is the time
To focus and enter
Into a new stage
A stage of expression

Edgar Boone

Take the genius out
Expand into the world
Transform it, change it

—∞—

August 26th, 2009

You came and you left
For a few hours I sensed
I sensed who I am
Then you left

Please come back
I want you here with me
Beloved Soul

Don't you see?
I am here with you
I am here
But distracted are you
Concentrate
Let me kiss your lips
To bring you back the love
You so much crave

Oh my beloved
I love you so much
Finally we are friends
We are ONE

It took us long
For striving you have been

I am honored, I am grateful
For the effort put forth

From where I am
Tears of Light came out of my being
For the joy of our reunion
For the love expressed and accepted

Oh beloved spirit, my soul
So much kindness
So much tenderness embraces me
We have become ONE
Interchangeable
Universal and individual
A human and a spirit
A human divine
An angel on earth

—⚹—

August 26th, 2009

Tears fell from my eyes
Tribute waters of the pain experienced
I have been consumed by the elixir of love
By my beloved friend, Shiva
And her tool, Kundalini
Companions for long
What do you bring to my life?
Feelings and more feelings
The intensity brings pain to my chest
To my body

Edgar Boone

What can I do?
Fight? NO!
Let go! YES!

Let it consume you, he said
I thought
Then I did

Now I am no one and someone
An instrument of our creator
A brother to my race

Cripple though I am
I try to come out
Though I barely can try

What can I say if I cannot even talk
What can I do if I can barely walk
It seems so easy for others
I wonder, why me? Why?

Now I am here
With little strength
Upset and wanting to jump out of my body
But I stay

It will adjust in time
To this new intensity of being, of feeling
As usual, when a new level comes
I experience deep pressure
Even more when the ego dies

I watched the whole process ensue
Like watching a murder

But this is of the ego
Let it rest in peace
His job is done
That of playing the game of the world

No more
Now, I'll give myself
The time to be
To feel, to love
To die in peace

August 28th, 2009 – 9:20 a.m.

I am in love
So in love
I am in love with creation
Creation is in love with me
Yes, yes, we are One
We are friends

August 29th, 2009 – 10:00 a.m.

I am here
Observing it all
Feeling it all
Letting myself be consumed
By divine fire
Until I am no more

Edgar Boone

August 29th, 2009

People go, people come
Some in fear, some in anger
Some sad, some happy
Some confused, some seemingly clear

I see them as atoms revolving around me
I, like a father, wait for their arrival
In those precious and short moments
When they open their eyes and they see me
We connect, we recognize each other

I tell them 'welcome my son'
'Welcome my daughter'
We re-unite

Until they go back to delusion
Living the drama of life
And I wait, with my heart open
Nurturing love through the cosmos
Until they come back
Opening their eyes for a second
To celebrate our reunion

They don't know it
But even in their dreamtime
I am there, always there
Like a mother with a child
Embracing them, caring for them
Until they open their eyes
Yes, when they open their eyes
It's such a joy to see each other
And remember our nature of Light

I am the father
These are my children
Revolving and evolving
Around the sun
My heart

—⁂—

August 30th, 2009 – 8:48 a.m.

You tell me you love me
And I say
I know what you mean
I love you too
This path has brought us together
We have merged
The metamorphosis is almost complete
We are loved, we are ONE

We look around
And we see our children
Our family
We are home
I am home
Home

—⁂—

August 30th, 2009

The more I travel
The more I absorb
The ways of the world

And the world absorbs me
We together dance
The drama of life
I am Shiva

―※―

August 30th, 2009

The elixir of love flows through my being
This thick and subtle substance
Feeds our children
Nurtures our babies
I am pleased
I am complete

―※―

August 30th, 2009 – 2:50 p.m.

Love
Sweet elixir of the universe
Made matter
Is what I am

―※―

August 30th, 2009

I can sense this sweet
And subtle presence
It's the source of it all
Manifested in matter
Through the pathway of light

Love in density
That's what I am

—⚜—

September 1st, 2009

Things are clearer
I see experiences past
The journey traveled
And not understood
I am a child in a world
That I barely understand

—⚜—

September 2nd, 2009 – 9:11 a.m.

I can sense thoughts flowing through my mind
I can hear angels singing praises to us all
Another one has arrived home
One of our members of Light
Made the transition
Through the struggle of human life
Tears in my eyes
Gratitude in my heart

—⚜—

September 2nd, 2009

There is no place like Home
There is no time like Now
There's no One but One

—⚜—

Edgar Boone

September 2nd, 2009

I contemplate
I feel this substance flow through me
This sea of magnificence, of love
It's re-gaining every space of my being
It is re-gaining that which was lost
My true nature of light

I hear angels sing
I hear their praise
I feel their joy
Their tenderness
Drums of creation
Heartbeat of the universe
I am It and It is me
I disappeared, I am no more
The sparks of the cosmos
Shines through this instrument

September 2nd, 2009

I am back
With tears in my eyes
I have landed on earth again
To care for my children
And re-unite with my lover

September 4th, 2009 – 11:19 p.m.

Love is
Love is all
Love is the substance that holds the universe together
Love is the Self-aware consciousness of the universe
Love is the sweet elixir that pervades all things

Love is warm, Love is firm
Love flows, Love burns
Love transcends, Love descends
Love is praised by angels
Love is desired by humans

Love is
Yes, Love is
Love is the rapture of the Gods
It is the ultimate experience of ascension

Love is
Love is manifested in attraction and repulsion
Love is the material of the Source
Love is feminine
Love is the mother
Fire is the father
Bring them together
And the universe is created
The Alpha and the Omega
The Beginning and the End

Edgar Boone

September 7th, 2009 – 12:45 a.m.

That
What is That?
That is the Source
That is Love
That is God
That is unnamable
That is
That is All
And All is That
I AM THAT
From which the vibration comes
THAT is the source
Of wisdom
Of truth
Of light

September 7th, 2009 – 9:06 a.m.

That is Love and Love is That
The Source vibrates its vibrations
It is Love
The Source creates its creations
Love is
The Source enjoys itself, by Love it does
Love is
Love can not
Not be
It covers every thing and every one
Love is

September 7th, 2009

THAT is God and God is THAT
I am THAT, perceiving THAT
I am THAT projecting
I am THAT intro-jecting
I am the Source and the creation
The Alpha and the Omega

―⁂―

September 10th, 2009 – 1:47 a.m.

Ohm, Ohm, Ohm
Ohm, Ohm, Ohm
I feel the vibration of life
I feel the living spirit flow through me
Through it All
Ohm, Ohm, Ohm
My brain synchronized with It
It merges
I feel its life flowing through my veins
It's the living thought
It is life

Ohm, Ohm, Ohm
I AM
(Silence)

―⁂―

September 10th, 2009 – 4:03 p.m.

I am water
I am the living fluid
Drink from my heart
The never ending well
The Source of It All

—⁂—

September 10th, 2009

In the water I am now
I'm totally immersed in Spirit
Baptized in your grace
I was swallowed

—⁂—

September 13th, 2009 – 8:25 a.m.

Submerged in the spirit water
My physical body is in pain
He is gone but he lives in me
I can feel the intensity of our being rising
Ascending into the Father
Our source

—⁂—

September 13th, 2009

We are One now
WE ARE
ARE
O (Alpha and Omega)

―⁂―

September 21st, 2009 – 9:30 p.m.

I do not seek
And I do not stop
I create as I flow
I remember the unseen
I sense all memories of past times
I carry the world in me
I AM the world

―⁂―

September 21st, 2009

If you do not remember me
It is because you are distracted

If you do not see me
It is because you don't look

If you do not hear
It is because you don't listen

If you do not feel me
It is because in your head you are

Just stop for a moment

And experience ME experiencing YOU
And experience YOU experiencing ME

Now WE did
ONE WE ARE

September 21st, 2009

See me
Touch me
Hear me
Taste me
Smell me
I am here
As real as you are
In flesh and bone
I have descended and merged
I am a human/divine

September 28th, 2009 – 1:12 p.m.

I feel drunk
Drunk of love
My chest is expanding
The sweet substance of love
Flows through my body, my soul
I am in Love
I am LOVE
I am the Presence
God in the flesh

October 4th, 2009 – 8:25 p.m.

Awakened
I am totally immersed
In the waters of life
I flow on this sea
It carries me
I have faith
This adventure
Has but just begun
Wonders and mysteries
Are opening to me

My mind
Is still in shock
My soul
Excited for the journey to come

What I thought reality was
Is but an illusion
What I thought was fiction
Is more real

My mind
Adjusting
To this new experience of living
More peaceful,
Calmer
But more physically intense

I live so much
In short periods of time
I opened my eyes

Edgar Boone

I looked around
I saw a world of sleepers
A world in motion
People desperate for solutions
In time
A new way
A new era
A new order
Will come
Yes
It will come

—⚘—

October 8th, 2009 – 4:59 p.m.

I hear you my children
I hear you
I can feel your pain
I listen to your prayers
I can sense your longing
You are not alone
Open your eyes
Please open them
It only takes your will
Your willingness to let go
Of all your beliefs
To see the truth
To be real
To be in reality
Present and in love

—⚘—

October 29th, 2009 – 6:32 p.m.

The light of the divine
Illuminates reality
I, observant of it all
Am a servant of its will

—⁂—

October 29th, 2009

I see the light of my body
I feel the vibration of my blood
I hear the sound of creation

—⁂—

October 29th, 2009

I am the Body of the universe
I am the Mind of the universe
I am the Spirit of the universe

—⁂—

November 9th, 2009 – 12:58 p.m.

Love, Love, Love
Love my dear
Let yourself explode in it
Let your pride be burned by it

Love, Love, Love
Love, Love, Love

Edgar Boone

Open your eyes
Open your ears
Open your heart
My dear Children
Let my elixir fill
The empty void of your despair
Let me guide you into a place
Of clarity and joy
One day, yes one day
You will remember
You will realize
That it has been you
Creating your own misery
Creating your own confusion

November 9th, 2009

The joy that I feel
When you look at me
It's enough payment for a thousand years

You are my children
You are my beloved

That's why I'm here
That's why I'm back

November 9th, 2009.

To see the light
Is to see
To see beyond light
Is to see me

To hear sounds
Is to hear

To hear beyond sound
Is to hear me
To experience beyond the senses
Is to experience your soul

To experience beyond your soul
Is to experience me
It is to lift the veil
Of the Wizard of Oz

―⁂―

November 9th, 2009

You come to me
You are afraid
Will you make it in the world?
I don't know my child
I don't know

―⁂―

November 9th, 2009 – 8:50 p.m.

I AM FREE
(Silence)

—⚇—

I am the one who sees
I am the one who hears
I am the one who feels
I am the one who tastes
I am the one who smells
I am the one who is aware
I am the one beyond awareness
I am beyond and above
I am here and below
I am that I am
I am the source and the effect
I am the beginning and the end
I AM

—⚇—

www.edgarboone.com

www.pathsofthesoul.com

Made in the USA
San Bernardino, CA
11 November 2014